# A WOMAN'S GUIDE TO
# SELF DEFENSE

## PRACTICAL, DIRECT
## MARTIAL ARTS FOR WOMEN

### BY VIC SHAYNE

■ ■ A WOMAN'S GUIDE TO SELF DEFENSE

The author, publisher and distributors are not responsible for any injury resultant from advice, hints, or techniques discussed or from any information contained in this book. This book is designed as a guidebook and not a training manual. Although the information and techniques have been proven effective as means of self defense, it takes diligent practice,with concentration, understanding, timing and knowledge to employ them effectively as a method of self defense. Techniques and other information contained herein may cause physical and other damages if improperly employed or in the act of practicing them. As such, it is advised that the reader seek professional, qualified instruction for his/her personal safety and for correct application of techniques, principles and suggestions. The reader assumes the responsibility to consult a trained instructor for proper execution of techniques and their consequences.

CREATIVE BUREAU, INC.
13326 S.W. 28 STREET, SUITE 102, FT. LAUDERDALE, FL 33330
USA

# ACKNOWLEDGEMENTS

To the people who made this book possible — my parents, my brother Gordon for his willing and able legal advice and to my partner, Janice.
Special thanks to Master Ji Young Song for our long-term friendship, his special attention and training. Also, thanks to Master Andrew Chung for teaching me meaning, purpose and mindfulness. Special thanks to Tasha and Joshua, who assisted me by demonstrating techniques, and to my good friends Dr. Gil Williams and Bettie Williams for their generous help and friendship. Much gratitude goes to Ruben Alfaro for the photographs contained in this book and to Janice Shayne and Ykisha Walker who posed as photographic subjects.
Lastly, here's to Diana Hunter!

# About
# The Author

Vic Shayne has been studying the martial arts for more than twenty years and has attained the degree of 3rd Dan Black Belt in the Korean art of Tae Kwon Do under Grandmaster Ji Young Song, National Champion of Korea and Chief Tae Kwon Do Instructor of the Korean Army. Shayne, who teaches a course on self defense for women, has also studied the Japanese martial art systems of Judo, Jujutsu (under Black Belt Hall of Fame Sensei Ernie Reynolds), Shotokan and the Chinese systems of Hakka Kuen, Tai Chi and Chin Na from Master Andrew Chung in Hollywood, Florida. Professionally, Vic Shayne earns his living as a writer and marketing consultant in Fort Lauderdale, Florida.

# Foreword

This volume, which provides women with a knowledge and understanding of self defense, is a valuable tool in helping readers achieve independence through strength. The martial arts offers a significant way to accomplish this goal, for at the heart of the ancient teachings is the philosophy that no one should ever have the right to control another against his/her will. However, the art of self defense goes far beyond the physical aspects. Therefore, only with a balanced mind and spirit can any technique be *optimally* engaged into use.

— Ji Young Song
8th Degree Tae Kwon Do Grandmaster
National Korean Middle Weight Champion
Chief Tae Kwon Do Instructor, Korean Army

## ORDER THIS BOOK FOR A FRIEND!!

Use this convenient form or a copy of it
to order additional copies of
**A WOMAN'S GUIDE TO SELF DEFENSE.**

☑ YES! I would like to order _____ copies of
A WOMAN'S GUIDE TO SELF DEFENSE at $12.95 per copy plus
$2 shipping and handling. (Florida residents add 78¢ sales tax per
book). Please remit check or money order (do not send cash). For bulk
orders, please write for our discount schedule.

Send book(s) to:

Name: _____

Address: _____

Apt.# _____

City_____ State _____ Zip _____

**SEND WITH PAYMENT TO:**
WOMEN'S PUBLICATIONS, INC.,
13326 SW 28 STREET, FT. LAUDERDALE, FLORIDA 33330

# Contents

*Through your own efforts and*
*determination*
*you can enjoy your independent*
*lifestyle to the fullest*
*— with skill and confidence.*

# CHAPTER ONE
## Introduction:
## Self Defense for Women

This book was written for women who live an independent lifestyle, whether by preference, or as a result of circumstances that have altered their lives — such as divorce, going back to school, marrying later in life, career choices, etc. This independence, which is relatively new in our culture, has brought with it situations that women now face in greater numbers — living alone, going out unescorted, driving alone, traveling alone, working late at the office (and sexual harrassment), walking or living alone on college campuses, and so on. Women's independence represents a giant step in social consciousness, but on the flip side, it has created opportunities for criminals looking for "easy prey." But the criminals need not have their way. As a woman, instead of restricting your independence, all you have to do is learn to take responsibility for your personal safety. This is the greatest enhancement of independence. This is TAKING CONTROL.

The mere title of this book, *A WOMAN'S GUIDE TO SELF DEFENSE,* suggests that there is a type of self defense for women that is different in some way from self defense techniques that may be employed by men. In a sense, this is true. Although martial arts exist in a genderless form, indifferent to sexual bias, there are many techniques, concepts and practices which are more adaptable by women than by men. Despite centuries of sexual bias, females are in many ways far more capable than their male counterparts to grasp the deeper concepts of martial arts and to apply them. Women, in general, tend to exhibit more patience for learning and possess more balanced ego than their male counterparts, thus allowing them to accept and control the power that comes with knowledge and mastery of techniques. On the other hand, generally speaking, females tend to lack naturally aggressive personalities advantageous for successful physical combat. Luckily, aggression may be acquired or mocked-up through practice and "stored away" until needed.

Each individual, according to his/her own talents, skills, abilities, potential and physical, spiritual and mental make-up, is unique enough to create his or her own specialty. For instance, a heavy-set person may use his weight to his advantage, or a smart woman may use her cunning to outwit an opponent. As we look at the martial arts as part of a system of physical, mental and spiritual balance, you will see that there is far more to self defense than just kicking, punching and throwing techniques. The purpose of self defense is to keep someone from harming you. The ways to carry out this objective are almost infinite, ranging from running away and hiding to using deadly force.

The common goal of martial arts, since its inception, is to utilize all the tools — physical and otherwise — available to the practitioner. And the martial arts, for those willing to commit themselves to employing them to their maximum benefit, should be studied in the context of a greater system. This takes patience, adaptability and an open mind.

This book takes a divergent approach to the typical study of self defense so that you can gain the most benefit from it instead of reading or studying concepts and techniques that have little practical use in the immediate sense.

One point that should be stated is that success comes through practice — physical and mental. It is ideal to have a practicing partner and even better to join a good martial arts school in which the instructor is a highly skilled, understanding and interested individual. If you join a good Kung Fu (Chinese), Karate (Japanese) or Tae Kwon Do (Korean) school, with an instructor who understands the mental aspects of martial arts, as well as the physical, you have a greater potential of acquiring the proper techniques used for kicking and striking. A good instructor can teach the role of balance, infighting and working with *chi* (internal energy). In addition, there are many seminars, books, videos and lectures at your disposal.

In the pages to follow, there are many secrets of self defense that you are not likely to learn in any one school without first committing yourself to years of dedicated training. The reason for this is simple. If you are reading this book, you need to be able to defend yourself NOW, not after two, three or ten years. To reap the ultimate benefit from the information provided in this book, you should not only practice the physical techniques laid out, but also, and with even more vigor, the mental and spiritual exercises, for this is the foundation of all success — increased awareness and the ability to control your body and emotions with your mind.

Today's martial arts styles take into consideration self defense moves (attack/counterattack practice); forms (a set of pre-determined moves against invisible or pretend opponents); sparring (exchanging kicks and punches with an opponent in a controlled atmosphere); and basics (the repeated practice of performing basic techniques either in-place or while moving forward and backward). All of these techniques are beneficial, on mental and physical levels, yet the art of self defense is empty without learning and practicing the art of building confidence and balance through mental and spiritual exercises. Thusly, you may perfect your technique as well as increase strength internally and externally. To illustrate this, all we have to do is listen to popular sports figures tell of how they play an entire game in their heads the night before the actual event occurs. Or, we can consider why we may dream of an incident and its outcome before it takes place. Or, why, before we go to the store, we often make a "mental list" of the items we want to buy. The point is, the use of the mental faculties in achieving physical goals is the key to success. The reason why these mental exercises are overlooked by so many martial arts teachers today is because these instructors are not aware or proficient in such exercises, are not interested in passing them on to their students, or are not qualified to be teaching martial arts.

# CHAPTER TWO
# In Search Of A Deeper Meaning

Martial arts is one of the most misunderstood, misinterpreted and misused phrases in our Western vocabulary. Over the short course of Western history, the term martial arts has developed into a phrase which is synonymous with self defense, including kicking, punching, grappling and throwing techniques. However, these techniques are only the *physical* aspects of a much deeper, much richer system; and to practice these techniques without an understanding and appreciation of the entire system from which they come is to perpetrate an injustice to the practitioner.

When we think of martial arts, we must think of it as an outgrowth of spirituality — an attempt to be balanced individuals for a greater spiritual purpose. In the next chapter we will see that martial arts developed out of a focused attempt to bring balance into the practitioner's life style — to keep one from living with either a too-physically oriented approach or a too-spiritually oriented approach. A sedentary life style needs to be balanced with physical activity as does a mentally focused life style. On the other hand, a life of physical labor must be balanced with mental exercise. And in all cases, all of life must be rooted in a deeper, spiritual meaning. The overindulgence in any one specific aspect of life creates a lack of balance. This out-of-balance state applies to much more than martial arts — it is the cause of unhappiness, over-excitedness, obesity, emaciation, brashness, timidity, sleepiness, insomnia and so on, covering the entire spectrum of dichotomies in the physical world. These dichotomies, or opposites, are known as *Yin* and *Yang* and are the components of a balanced world. On a spiritual level, it is our goal, according to the spiritual masters, to ride the middle ground and avoid falling into the state of imbalance which is caused by lust, vanity, attachment, greed or anger — negative emotions.

Relating this philosophy, or way of life, specifically to the practice of martial arts, we come to realize that the secret to optimal employment of any self defense technique is to use inner strength and energy known as *chi*, *ki*, or *gi* — and balance this energy with physical and mental energies. By employing only physical techniques as self defense, without consideration of mind and spirit as well, one exhibits an unbalanced act.

Balance is the key to all life, according to the ageless wisdom of the East. Balance — the middle path — allows the practitioner to remain calm in the face of danger, to flow with the difficulties of life, knowing when to resist and when to let go, knowing when to give and when to receive, and how to control one's body, mind and spirit. The practice of balance is a way of life, a way of looking at one's world and a way of approaching problem-solving, obstacles and adversity.

ECK Master Paul Twitchell wrote, "Spiritual development must be balanced in order to make an inspiring, happy and useful experience in the physical body. To provide this, the spiritual travelers, the Masters, found that there must be practice of the spiritual principles in this world which lead to happiness, livingness, kindness, tolerance, lovingness and success. Without the test of material results, there is the danger of the spiritual becoming a romantic

14

emotion, unable to stand up to the stress of ordinary life. We should make full use of our spiritual development, of our faith on both the spiritual and physical levels. In this way, we safeguard ourselves against the lack of balance and become a source of benefit and inspiration to others."

Twitchell also wrote, "The knowledge of maintaining life comes through the balance of the attitude towards love. Since we dwell constantly in the great stream of life, we must be taught to balance ourselves within it. Man cannot escape the negative forces nor the positive forces, so he must make the effort to have a well-adjusted outlook on the middle path.

"Hence, the teachings of the great [spiritual] Masters of the world were neither fanatics, nor weaklings, but strong-willed in God, seeing their own weaknesses and strength; pitting and balancing good and evil in their lives in the two streams of consciousness flowing through their worlds, the subjective and objective.

"Buddha portrayed this in his wonderful teachings to mankind. 'Travel the middle path,' he said. Now, herein, on the middle path, the consciousness of man eventually becomes the impersonal atom of pure intelligence, and the seeker is no longer himself.

"His consciousness is not the angry, cascading stream of negativism, but in pure balance with the positive, like some broad, placid river. The usual phrases, protesting or fearful, that went through his mind, are no longer tormenting him, and in their place are large, serene thoughts which come floating along the river of consciousness like nobly colored barges."[2]

The balance of fighting skills, religion, healing and philosophy are the elements which were consolidated into the martial arts.[4]

To discover some of the true power and meaning of martial arts, we need to explore the common origin of all Eastern-based martial arts systems and find the secrets which allow internal energy to be generated into external force for health and healing as well as self defense. To do this, you must have patience and be able to adapt a non-judgmental, balanced attitude to a foreign mode of thinking and living; for in this patient attitude, you will open yourself up to accepting concepts enabling you to generate your physical techniques with focused, internal force.

By studying the origin of martial arts, you will see that Eastern religion, mind-set and spirituality, entwined with the twists and turns of history, have created a way of life of which martial arts is a only small part. The original purpose of martial arts systems was to enhance the spiritual nature of the practitioner by keeping his body and mind engaged in healthy exercise.

Although the origin of martial arts is clouded in the misty past, we do know that fighting techniques, exercise, nutrition, medicine, meditation, contemplation, attitudes, philosophy, Eastern religion and life style are all inseparably intertwined— part of a greater system which has unfortunately become bastardized and watered down in the fast-paced, Western world. With an in-depth understanding of the laws of balance and nature, the true master of the martial arts uses an eclectic universe of "tools" to ply his trade. He knows not only where to strike an adversary, but also what time of day leaves specific targets of the human body most vulnerable. He also takes into consideration his adversary's proximity to bodies of water, body type and more. Much of this sounds abstract and far-fetched, but the more you understand the infinite systems of balance, the more you can use them to your advantage, not only to become a better martial artist, but to become a more enriched individual.

If any instructor, including a "master," is without a full understanding and appreciation of these mental and spiritual aspects of the martial arts, he is incapable of passing them on to his students. To further elaborate on this, ironically we find that it is also true that even if master instructors were well-versed in the all-encompassing aspects of the martial arts, they would be, at best, reluctant to pass the secret teachings onto their students. One of the reasons for this is that Western life style and mind-set are different than in the East. As Westerners, we tend to focus so much time and energy in earning a living and trying to cope with demanding schedules that we cannot devote ourselves to full immersion into anything. As a result, martial arts is relegated to either sport or hobby, but rarely, if ever, a way of life as it was first intended. As an extension of this Western mode of thinking, the goal of martial arts training frequently becomes to obtain a black belt or title of some sort, and the most worthy goal — to become a healthier, more proficient person — becomes lost in the shuffle.

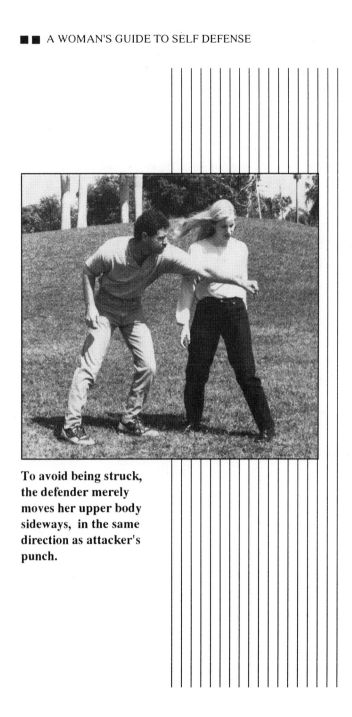

To avoid being struck, the defender merely moves her upper body sideways, in the same direction as attacker's punch.

# CHAPTER THREE

# Humble Beginnings — A Brief History

Around 500 A.D., when India, the source of Buddhism, was considered the seat of Spirituality by the Chinese, it became common practice for the emperors of China to import and export priests for the enlightenment of their people. One such priest, Da Mo, was considered to have been a *bodhisattva* — an enlightened being who dedicated his life to helping others break free from the negative passions which held them down in this physical plane of existence.

Da Mo came to China around 527 A.D. during the reign of Emperor Liang Wu of the Liang dynasty. However, after meeting with the emperor, Liang Wu disagreed with Da Mo's Buddhist theory (which was one of many Buddhist schools of thought). As such, Da Mo departed and traveled onward to the Shaolin Temple in Henan province, where he spent the rest of his life.

According to Dr. Yang Jwing-Ming, when Da Mo arrived at the temple, he saw that the monks were generally in poor physical condition because of their lack of exercise. He was so perplexed by the fact that the monks were weak, in ill-health and could do very little for themselves that he went into a period of contemplation for nine years until he came out with a solution and wrote two books. One of these works, the *Yi Gin Ching* (Muscle Development Classic) survives to this day and contains exercises which are a form of *Wai Dan* (external-internal *Chi Kung*), focusing on the use of concentration to develop and increase Chi power. This specialized training was integrated into the martial arts forms.[3]

Dr. Yang Jwing-Ming explains, for more than 1,400 years, Shaolin Temple monks have trained using the Da Mo *Wai Dan* exercises. Such exercises used to be secret and have only recently come into renown and put to popular use by the Chinese people. The Shaolin monks practice these exercises, *Chi Kung* (pronounced chee kung), not just to circulate chi and improve their health, but also to build their internal power by concentrating chi to affect the appropriate

**Da Mo**

muscles. Chi Kung is a practice that has been utilized by the Chinese for thousands of years to control and stimulate the energy within oneself for the benefit of healing and vitality. In the course of evolution, Chi Kung has been incorporated into martial arts forms to enhance their power.

## SECRET TEACHINGS
### Are the Secrets in the Forms?

Chi Kung experts, until very recently, would only teach their own sons or a select few they trusted, keeping their martial arts knowledge secret and contained. Moreover, many of the secret techniques were developed and enhanced by Buddhist or Taoist monks who would not spread their teachings outside their own temples.

Secrecy has long been one of the hallmarks of martial arts. In China, most forms of fighting, with specific techniques, originated as family systems, taught only to family members. Even when the scope of students was expanded to include a whole village, some of the secrets were still held back, reserved solely for the immediate family.[5]

Master George Dillman, an active proponent of pressure point fighting, explains, "In traditional Japanese bujutsu (the warrior arts of the samurai) instruction was divided into three levels. There was *shoden*, or basic teaching, *chuden*, or intermediate teaching, and *okuden*, or secret teaching. Only a very few were entrusted with the okuden material. Everyone else was deliberately excluded."[6]

With the advent and practice of forms (a series of movements against an imaginary opponent) designed by masters, a practitioner could not only maintain and perfect his art, but also keep the details of his exact actions a secret.

According to Dillman, "It is not possible to look at a kata [form] and see what is really going on, unless one is trained in the deepest aspects of the art. In meaning, kata movements change point of view constantly — one moment showing the attack, the next showing the defense. The kata follows a particular sequence, yet this often has no relationship to the sequence to be used in a fight. The performance of kata is continuous, but the meaning is interpreted in smaller units. The directions of movements in kata steps may appear to represent the directions from which various attacks originate, when in fact they tell the practitioner at what angle to position himself in relation to the attacker."[7]

So, we see that many of the secret techniques, stances, movements and strategies of the martial arts were, and are, hidden inside the forms. It is ironic, then, that most martial artists today in the West show little interest in mastery of the forms, but display much more enthusiasm in practicing sparring techniques or breaking boards and bricks for demonstration. These practices require very little in the way of mental exercise, or the use and development of chi.

Throughout the centuries, China, Japan and Korea all developed what are today's most popularly recognized forms of martial arts systems. Looking deeply enough into any one of these systems will reveal that each has at its roots a sense of deep concentration, emphasis on mental, spiritual and physical health, commitment to perfecting fighting skills and strategies, and a dedication to moral righteousness.

It cannot be overstated that the root of all strength and proficiency in these systems stem from the mastery of internal energy — *chi, gi* or *ki.*

# CHAPTER FOUR
## Anatomy of An Opponent

Recognizing that the practice of manipulating the life-force, or chi, is a double-edged sword, based on the philosophy of Yin and Yang (the law of opposites and balance), we see those same points of the body which are stimulated for healing may also be attacked, in the application of martial arts techniques. A knowledge of healing arts such as acupuncture, acupressure, or reflexology for instance, can be employed to damage as well as to restore vitality. In either case, the same "chi channels" are affected.

At the source of the ancient Chinese practice of *Chi Kung* is a medical practice concerned with the flow of chi, or energy, throughout the body, giving an individual life, health and vitality. When chi becomes blocked as a result of illness or trauma, energy to a specific area of the body is restricted and that area loses its ability to function to its fullest potential. Just as a blocked artery may cause the heart to fail, a blocked chi channel will cause some corresponding body part to falter in its proper function.

Dr. Yang Jwing-Ming explains, "A chi channel is a major connector of the internal organs with the rest of the body. These channels frequently are co-located with major nerves or arteries, but the correspondence is not complete, and it seems that they are neither nerves nor blood vessels, but simply routes for chi. There are twelve main channels and two major vessels, which are also commonly called

channels. Along these channels are found the 'cavities' sometimes known as acupuncture points, which can be used to
stimulate the entire system."[8]

In addition to acupuncture, chi may be stimulated by
a wide array of influences, including but not limited to
sound, food, breathing, nature (wind direction, seasons, hu-
midity, time of day, air pressure, etc.), and even proximity

to bodies of water such as lakes or oceans. Many of these influences may seem strange to you, but the point may be best illustrated when considering a drunk person. It is obvious that a drunk's chi system is impaired by the way he acts, resultant of an excess of alcohol in the bloodstream — his brain is not functioning normally, his speech is slurred, his pupils are dilated, his actions are clumsy and his thought processes are irrational. An intimate knowledge of the unseen, but present, affects upon an opponent's chi gives you a great advantage over him in the event of a confrontation.

Chi channels correspond to, and affect, specific organs in the human body and run along "meridians." Therefore, the stimulation of one of the chi channels will have an effect on one of the organs which are related to the same energy pathway. In this way, it is possible to stimulate or interrupt chi flow to the kidney, for instance, by affecting a corresponding impulse on the leg. For a complete diagram of these chi channels, consult a book on acupuncture.

The seat, or source, of chi in the body is in an area that the Chinese refer to as the lower *Dan Tien*, located in the lower abdomen, one and a half inches below the navel. By concentrating one's thoughts on the lower Dan Tien, one can increase chi. Further concentration can move or direct this chi to parts of the body in need of stimulation. And, with even further concentration, one can direct this reservoir of chi up from the lower Dan Tien and out of one's body to be directed at another individual for the purposes of healing or self defense. In healing, the chi may be used to restore chi flow in a patient; and in self defense, the direction of chi may be used to interrupt the chi flow in an opponent. The ancient Chinese art known as *Tai Chi Chuan* contains forms (exercises) that stimulate and generate chi which have both therapeutic value and martial arts applications.

**The chi system is under the control of the mind**, which means that anyone has the potential to master it, using it to heal, protect or deploy in self defense. Through meditation, the masters of the martial arts have been able to strengthen their ability to use the mind and manipulate internal and external forces.

"In Chi Kung training, concentration is the key to success. By concentrating attention on the abdomen and doing certain exercises, chi is generated and circulated throughout the body. This leads to the development of extra energy and its more efficient use, allowing the martial artist to strike with tremendous power and to resist the penetration of an opponent's power into his body. The amount of chi that can be generated is determined largely by the person's ability to concentrate."[9]

It should be mentioned here that, as in the practice of yoga, a true understanding of breathing is the cornerstone of regulating and working with chi, as correct breathing fills the body with this life force. Combined with the optimized mental acuity, knowledge of chi channels and cavities (discussed below) enable even the weakest of fighters to disable their opponents with minimal amounts of force. In this light, a 115-pound female can easily disable and incapacitate her 240-pound attacker with just the right placement of a finger.

## CAVITIES — USING PRESSURE POINTS

Cavities, commonly known as acupuncture points, are spots where chi channels are particularly close to the surface of the skin. They can often be felt as small depressions and are more sensitive than other parts of the body, as protective sheaths of muscle around them are less thick. These cavities are used in acupuncture as well as points of attack in martial arts. According to Dr. Ming, acupuncture recognizes more than 700 cavities, yet only a little more than a hundred of these are used by martial artists. The application of power to one of these cavities can cause pain, numbness, unconsciousness, damage to one of the internal organs or even

## Pressure Points
## To Be Struck

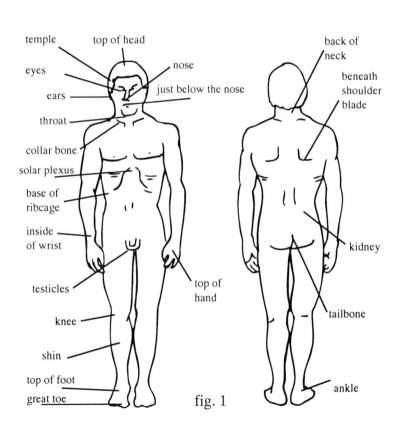

temple    top of head

nose

eyes

just below the nose

ears

throat

collar bone

solar plexus

base of ribcage

inside of wrist

testicles

knee

shin

top of foot

great toe

top of hand

back of neck

beneath shoulder blade

kidney

tailbone

ankle

fig. 1

death. For example, if the cavity on the heart channel located under the armpit was to be struck in the right direction with the right amount of force, the result would be a fatal heart attack. With the extreme seriousness and potential of this art, we can see why such knowledge has been kept in secrecy,

## Pressure Points
## To Be Rubbed

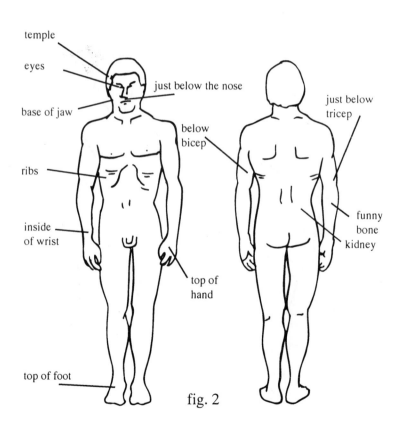

fig. 2

reserved only for the most discriminating, worthy and re-sponsible student. We can also see why most of the martial arts have been "watered down" for consumption in the West where there is little or no regard for a tradition of disciplined study and spirituality.

For a full understanding of the chi systems within the human body, it is strongly recommend that you read *Chi Kung,*

## Pressure Points
## To Be Pressed

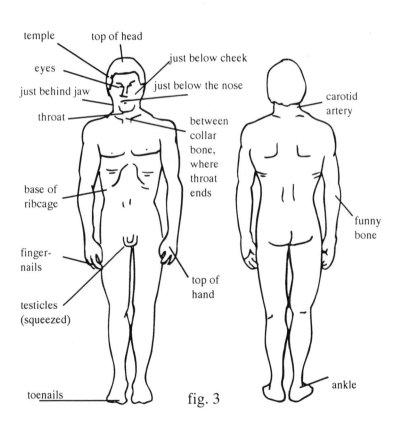

fig. 3

*Health & Martial Arts,* by Dr. Yang Jwing-Ming. For the purposes of this book, we will not delve too deeply into the intricacies of these systems, as we try to focus our attention more on immediate issues of self-defense practices. Therefore, let us progress into a general understanding of human anatomy and how to incorporate this knowledge into your self defense "arsenal."

## WHERE TO STRIKE

Based on what we have learned about chi cavities and channels, it is obvious that a well-placed strike has more effect than a hard strike that lands indiscriminately on the body. To

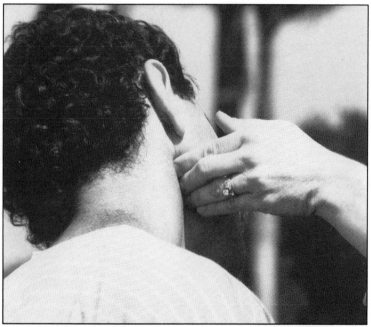

**Without much force, a pressure point may be pressed, causing pain in a tender area, allowing you to control your attacker with just the touch of a finger.**

**The eyes are an extremely sensitive and
vulnerable target.**

expound on this, it is also true that technique is far more
important in a physical confrontation than size or brute force.
As such, the largest, strongest man in the world could not
defeat a martial arts master (male or female) in a fight. Keep
this in mind when you consider that most men are larger and
stronger than you. A little understanding, patience and practice will show you that advantage comes in the form of
knowing how to apply techniques correctly, with concentration, timing, direction, force and accuracy.

Pressure points, which are cavities, are attacked
through one of three different ways: 1). striking (fig. 1); 2).
massaging or rubbing (fig. 2); and 3). pressing (fig. 3). You
must study which pressure points are affected by which
methods of stimulation and at what angle they must be

struck, otherwise, you'll greatly decrease your efficacy.

For the purposes of this book, you will have to pursue a more complete knowledge of pressure points and cavities from other sources (consult the reference list at the end of this book). For the sake of practicality, let's look at some of the most vulnerable body points and how to attack them. By practicing with a partner (without making contact) or on a dummy, you will be able to improve your aim, making it possible to strike a specific cavity at will. All of the areas in fig. 1 are susceptible to striking, whereas those targets in figure 2 should be rubbed; and areas in figure 3 should be pressed for greatest effect. The most renowned sensitive spots on the body are the eyes, nose and testicles. However, if one of these areas are not accessible, many more are at your disposal, including the throat, shins, knees and carotid artery by employing one of the three manipulations mentioned previously — striking, massaging or pressing.

Areas susceptible to rubbing include the area behind the triceps, the "funny bone" and the back of the hand, among others. By pressing, you can attack pressure points on the finger nails, above the upper lip and the carotid artery.

# CHAPTER FIVE

# Hands, Feet & Other Objects — Tools for Self Defense

Many of the techniques and postures used in the martial arts are derived from the self defense techniques of wild animals such as monkeys, cats, tigers, bears, cranes, etc.

Although we have two hands and two feet, as martial artists, we realize that there are many more weapons that can

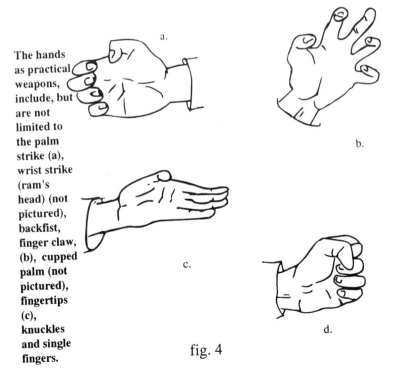

**The hands as practical weapons, include, but are not limited to the palm strike (a), wrist strike (ram's head) (not pictured), backfist, finger claw, (b), cupped palm (not pictured), fingertips (c), knuckles and single fingers.**

a.

b.

c.

d.

fig. 4

## fig. 5

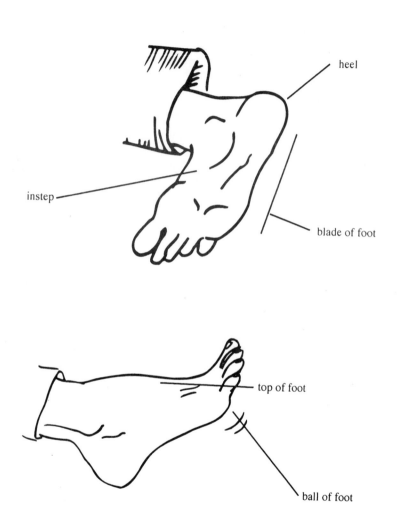

heel

instep

blade of foot

top of foot

ball of foot

**The foot as a weapon. You can use your heel, ball of foot, top of foot or instep as striking, tripping, sweeping or scraping tools.**

be fashioned out of them (fig. 4). The hand can be used to strike with the fist, heel of the palm, wrist, backfist, finger claw, cupped palm, fingertips, knuckles and single fingers. The feet (fig. 5) can be used to strike with the heel, ball of

**Using the head for butting, either backwards or forwards.**

fig. 6

fig. 7

**The elbow can be used in an upward, sideways or backwards motion and can deliver a powerful strike in an upright or downward manner.**

foot, top of foot or instep. Additionally, in your defense, you may use your weight, your hips, your head (fig. 6), legs, elbows (fig. 7), knees (fig. 8), fingernails (fig. 9), teeth, lungs (for screaming) or any object that is handy, such as an umbrella, a stick, a belt, sand, gravel, books, a telephone, chairs, etc.

With the repeated practice of mind or contemplative exercises, you may train yourself in the habit of thinking clearly. In this calm, collected state, you should have the

fig. 8

**Knees can be thrust into the groin of an attacker, into the thigh or into the head.**

presence of mind to determine which self defense "tool, " as well as which combination of techniques is best for the situation at hand.

**Fingernails may be used to gouge eyes, or to press on pressure points. The fingernail may be used to pinch or clamp down on the attacker's own fingernail (applied on the cuticle with downward pressure; see fig. 23, page 70).**

fig. 9

# CHAPTER SIX
# Striking
# Techniques

Effective punching and kicking is not a matter of gender or genetics, but rather a matter of training. As a female, if you become proficient in kicking and punching techniques, there is a great possibility that you will surprise an attacker with

your ability enough to gain a quick advantage. Why? The kind of human being who preys upon others has a low self-esteem and is looking for an easy victim, not a hard fight — it's the bully mentality.

Prior to practicing any striking techniques involving the head, neck, arms, hands, legs, feet or joints of any kind, it is strongly advised that the practitioner engage in stretching exercises. (See the chapter called "Stretching Exercises").

**In all four kicks which are noted in this book, each one begins with the rapid jerking of the knee to an upright position.**
**(This motion is in itself a strike — a knee strike).**

**knee strike**
fig. 10

## KICKING

In the previous chapter, we discussed where to strike, based on the pressure points on the human body. Now let's take a look at basic kicking. To illustrate the effectiveness of a well-placed kick aimed at an attacker's knee, consider what happens to a 6-foot, eight-inch tall, 300-pound football player when he sustains a knee injury. All of his might, all of his meanness and all of his agility disappears in the blink of an

**The front kick utilizes the instep, ball of the foot or the top of the foot as its striking surface. The kick is either snapped at its target, scraped downward, or thrust forward. Pictured below is a front kick using the instep. By using this portion of the foot, it's hard to miss the target.**

fig. 11

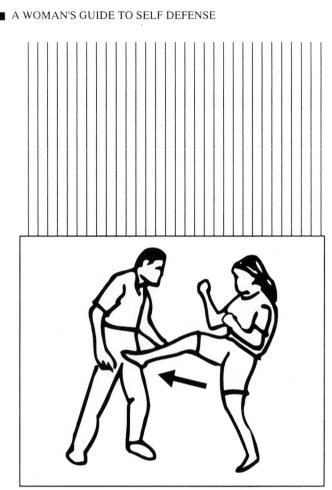

**Front kick to the groin or lower abdomen.**

eye as he clutches his injured knee in his hands or lies on the field gripped in pain, totally immobile. He has to be carried off the field, sometimes on a stretcher. And, this injury occurs by accident, in the course of regular play. Just think of the potential that you have to defend yourself by disabling your attacker with a well-placed, *intended* kick!

There are a number of ways to kick, but in this

volume, we will concentrate only on four basic kicks, known as the front, back, side and roundhouse kicks. All of these kicks (fig. 10 - 14) begin by bringing your knee and thigh parallel to the ground. In fact, this move in itself can be used as a strike (to the groin, for instance).

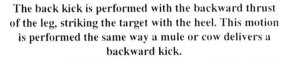

**The back kick is performed with the backward thrust of the leg, striking the target with the heel. This motion is performed the same way a mule or cow delivers a backward kick.**

**On the kicking foot, your heel is the first surface to strike, so keep your toes pulled back toward your body.**

fig. 12

43

In the front kick (fig. 11), the leg is fully thrusted outward so that the target is struck either with the top of the foot or with the ball of the foot (keep your toes pulled back toward your body — do not point them toward your opponent). In the back kick (fig. 12), with your back toward the attacker and looking over your shoulder, the leg is thrusted out directly behind you, as if imitating the kick of a cow or horse. The striking portion of your foot is the heel and your toes should be pulled back. When performing the side kick (fig. 13), turn sideways to your opponent then thrust your leg out to the side, striking him with the blade or side of the foot. Again,

**The side kick is effective in disabling the knee or leg of an attacker. A shin bone may be broken with minimum force using the blade of the foot.**

Side kick to the hip. Note the full extension of the
kicking leg. The force of the blow is aimed directly into
the target, with the hands positioned for optimal
balance.

keep your toes pointed toward you. The roundhouse kick requires you to torque your body sideways with your knee up, and thrust into the target while extending your leg, striking with either the top or ball of the foot (toes pulled back).

fig. 13

**The sidekick uses the blade of the foot as the striking surface and is thrust out from the side of the body (with your side facing the opponent). The sidekick is highly effective when placed on the knee or shins.**

fig. 14

**The roundhouse kick, utilizing the ball of the
foot for thrusting. Keep your toes pulled back to
expose the ball of your foot — do not strike with
the toes landing first.**

Note: on the front and roundhouse kicks, the top of
the foot can be used to strike softer and wider targets such
as the face, back or abdomen, while the ball of the foot can
be used for all of these same soft areas, plus smaller, specific
target areas such as the ribs, groin, kidneys, etc. To
strategically aim your kicks and strikes, it is important to
look at the target area; otherwise, if your opponent moves or
shifts position, you are liable to miss entirely.

Do not make the mistake of performing only a single
kick and then expect to walk away from a confrontation.
Follow up the kick with several more hand or foot techniques
until you are safe from injury. Although we see a lot of fancy

**Roundhouse kick used to strike and disable the knee.**

kicks in the movies, it is actually best to kick low (from the chest down) than high. The higher you kick, the less control and force accompanies the impact of your foot upon its target.

## HAND/ELBOW TECHNIQUES
Generally speaking, the hands provide a much more precise strike than the feet. That's because we work with our hands since birth to perform every kind of chore imaginable. Our hand-eye coordination is natural, whereas an excellent foot-eye coordination is usually the result of specific training of the feet and legs.

There are several schools of thought in regard to the

48

position of the fisted hand in the striking mode. Master George Dillman is a proponent of the "three-quarters" punch, in which the fist is at a 45-degree angle to the ground upon striking. In the Korean (and most Karate) styles, the knuckles are parallel to the ground. And in most Chinese styles, the knuckles are at a right angle to the ground. The Chinese explanation for the way they position the fist is that it can easily be retracted after the punch is delivered and can be quickly readied to strike again. This method allows the body to remain covered by the elbow and arm, as in this position,

The elbow, which is an extremely hard, bony surface, can be used effectively from several directions: thrust upwards, sideways, downward, or towards the rear. This technique may be used with the forearm instead of the elbow as well.

fig. 15

49

A series of strikes makes an effective defense. One example would be to first butt your opponent with your head (a), then strike the groin with your knee (b), then follow up with a palm heel (or elbow) strike to the face (c), jaw, neck, etc.

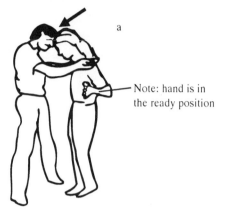

Note: hand is in the ready position

(c) Bring your striking hand upwards inside the opponent's arms and thrust upwards with your weight shifting in the same direction. But do not allow your feet to leave the ground by overextending or lunging.

fig. 16

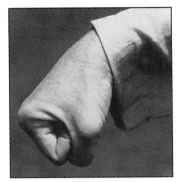

Above, incorrect fist. Note the
way the wrist is bent, lending no
support to the fist.

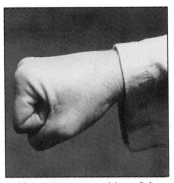

Above, correct position of the
wrist. Note how the wrist and
fist are on a straight line.

it is not flailing or bent away. This gives you protection
against being hit while you are striking. With right angle and
45-degree angle fists, the bones in the arm are in a natural
position at the moment the punch is executed. With the
typical Karate, parallel punch, the bones in the arm all but
cross each other upon execution, which weakens the impact
of the blow, as the fist has a lessened support structure
behind it.

The striking surface of the fist is the first two knuckles,
on the index and middle fingers. The wrist must be kept
straight and never bent. A bent wrist can easily fold, sprain
or break, on the impact of the strike. If the wrist is bent, the
fist has no support. In all cases, be sure to keep your thumb
outside of your fingers, not tucked in beneath them. To hit
specific pressure points, you may use a modified fist in
which the knuckle of the index or middle finger is extended
and employed as a penetrating tool. Because the size of the
pressure point, as a target, is relatively small, a single knuckle
will be able to reach that point and drive into it in a way that
a regular fist cannot.

Another way of using the fist is commonly referred to as the backfist. Here, the fist is used in a backhanded motion just as you would swing a tennis racket with the backhand. The striking surface is the two knuckles of the index and middle fingers with a clenched fist. The backfist (fig. 17) is very effective in a couple of ways. For one, the technique, when applied in a spinning fashion, carries an element of surprise. To execute the spinning backfist, it initially appears to the opponent that you are retreating — as you are turning away from him, you swing your arm around with a backhand motion, while turning the direction of your body 180 degrees and your head 360 degrees, and land your

**The backfist, using the first two knuckles as the striking surface, is a powerful technique, especially to the face, between the nose and upper lip, on the nose itself, or on the temple.**

fig. 17

blow. In this case, you are actually stepping *into* the attacker and not away from him, as it initially appears. Thus the element of surprise. (In more advanced kicking techniques, this same element of surprise can also be accomplished with a spinning hook kick.)

**TAKING ADVANTAGE:**
**Above: Woman reacts to offender reaching for breasts — If someone is**
**groping, grabbing or touching you and you do not want him to, instead of**
**struggling to block or remove his hand from your body, you may instead take**
**quick, easy advantage of him by forcefully striking him in the face while his**
**hands are preoccupied. To reiterate in other words...Without training and**
**practice, out of reflex, a woman will naturally react to being groped by**
**struggling to get the offender's hand off her person. With practice, however,**
**while the offender's hands are "busy," you can disable him with a strike to the**
**eyes, nose, temple, upper lip or ears. If you decide to strike back, do it with**
**force and confidence. Never fear that the offender will become angry with you,**
**because this will deter you from defending yourself. Your defense must be**
**quick, powerful and effective. Do not slap an offender across the face. You**
**have the power and ability to disable him and it does not take much more than**
**practice and precision to do this. Strength and force is secondary to technique.**

In addition to using your fists and arms as weapons, you can use fingers for poking, scratching, pushing, pulling, grabbing, twisting and pressing.

The elbow, which is an extremely hard, bony surface, can be used effectively from several directions (fig. 15).

Whenever using hand or elbow techniques, be sure to aim your strike at one of the pressure points discussed earlier and in combination with subsequent strikes. One technique quickly following another should be employed because, by hitting combinations of pressure points, you will do much greater damage to your opponent's chi system than performing a single strike. Moreover, unless expertly placed, with exacting force, angle and timing, a single strike will usually not be enough to disable an attacker.

There are many combinations of techniques that work effectively. One example (fig. 16) would be to first butt your opponent with your head (a), then strike the groin with your knee (b), then follow up with a palm heel (or elbow) strike to the face (c), jaw, neck, etc. Practice combinations always, not just one technique at a time.

Strikes with the feet or hands may be used from any position, whether seated, standing or lying. However, the most powerfully delivered techniques are dealt while in the standing position, with the proper, balanced stance (see the chapter on Stances).

# Blocking

Blocking is one of the most natural reactions we have, so we won't spend too much time on this area. The operative thought here, as any boxer will tell you, is to keep your hands covering your body. Keep your hands and arms relaxed so that they can move quickly and your energy will be saved for the block and not wasted on making your arm muscles tense. Also, keep your hands in front of you, with your elbows, not

**Low (down) Block. The low block is executed by sweeping your arm and fist across your body to deflect a low kick, punch or grab.**

fig. 18

touching, but covering, your body. Blocking, in and of itself, is rarely enough of an action to defend yourself, however, it can keep an attacker's strike from reaching your body.

Practice blocking and punching (or kicking) at the same time: This is a highly effective technique, as you grant the attacker no time to prepare for your counter move. Also, practice sidestepping (you may not need to waste your energy blocking) then counterstriking.

There are three basic kinds of blocks, including low blocks (fig. 18) (against strikes to the lower body), and

**Middle Block.** To execute this block, move the arm, with the forearm at a 45 degree angle to the ground, across your body, stopping a little past your face, in front of your body.
Your fist should be just below eye level.

fig. 19

High Block: The high block protects blows to the head, using the forearm to deflect a strike with an object or a fist. Keep your forearm bent at a 45 degree angle, with the fist only a couple of inches above and away from your head.

fig. 20

middle blocks (fig. 19) (against attacks to the middle body, neck, face, ribs, stomach), and high blocks (fig. 20) (against blows to the head). The most effective blocks land on pressure points on the arm of your opponent while his strike is coming toward you. If done with precision and force, your block by itself could disable the arm of your opponent instantly. It is also possible to block then strike with the same hand. For instance, if an attacker attempts a strike to your face, you may, in a "one-two" motion, block his hand and rapidly follow up with a backfist to his face.

# CHAPTER SEVEN
## Stances

The way you stand, if properly balanced and grounded, will add power to your striking techniques, as well as provide a better defense against being pushed, pulled or knocked over. Although we are used to seeing fighters bouncing around in the movies, most of this is for show. In actuality, the more you bounce up in the air, the less grounded you are, making you susceptible to being pulled or thrown off balance. On the other end of the spectrum, a very wide stance can lock you into position, making it difficult and cumbersome to move quickly. Therefore, the best stance for fighting is the "natural stance" in which your knees are slightly bent, about shoulder-distance apart, with your pelvis slightly thrust forward, and with your body turned three-quarters to your opponent.

The natural stance is ideal for kicking because you are able to shift your weight quickly onto either leg, as well as being able to turn, advance and retreat with ease.

If you are in-close with your opponent, your stance should be a bit wider, with your knees bent slightly more than in the natural stance; this way, you will have a lower center of gravity.

Most martial arts schools practice balancing exercises which enhance your stances, among providing other practical benefits. You can do these on your own by practicing standing on one foot and moving the other in large and small circles in the air. You will also increase your balance by practicing kicking and hand techniques while moving forward, backward and sideways.

From a "natural stance," you may move with
balance and agility while striking. Weight
should be distributed evenly on both legs.

When delivering a strike, your weight should be
behind the thrusting hand, knee, head or leg. However, be
sure to recover rapidly so that you are ready to strike again.

Never overextend yourself or lunge at your target.
This could result in your being pulled, tripped, pounced upon
or thrown. If you lunge and miss, you may not have another

opportunity to strike a second time.

Always keep your feet beneath you. This is in line with a previous warning against lunging or overextending. When your feet and legs are not beneath you, you are off balance and can be moved at will by your opponent. The most forceful techniques are delivered with a fully balanced stance, as the flow of energy from your blow is what causes the most damage, not your weight behind the blow.

## OBSERVE YOUR
## OPPONENT'S STANCE

By studying proper stances, you will be able to recognize off-balance stances — and this is advantageous to you in several ways. Firstly, if your opponent has all of his weight on his back leg, this would be the best leg for you to kick, as it has the most stress on it and will break the easiest. If your opponent is leaning forward, he can be pulled off balance, toward you. In this case, you can pull him into one of your hand or knee strikes, for instance. If your opponent has a very wide stance, his groin will be exposed and vulnerable to a strike. If he stands upright, he will have a higher center of gravity and will be vulnerable to a strike to the face, for instance, with the heel of your hand.

As a mental exercise, try observing people all the time, whether you are at work, at the mall, at restaurants, parties, etc. You should begin to notice how people walk, how they shift their weight and how they balance and unbalance themselves. With persistent observation, you may also see that certain body types are carried in similar fashion. Likewise, many personality types carry themselves in specific ways. For instance, many brash individuals expose their chests as they stick them out. Insecure people tend to "close" themselves up, keeping their hands and arms closer to their bodies. A good book on psychology and body language should be helpful as a guide to personality traits exhibited through unconscious carriage of the head, hands and shoulders. While it is unwise to guess a person's next move or motives by the way he carries himself, it can be of great advantage to learn where the opponent's stress points and exposed targets are.

# CHAPTER EIGHT
# Grappling, Wrestling & Struggling

One of the most frequently considered (and asked) questions women have regarding male attackers is: How could I possibly win in a struggle with a man who is much stronger than me? This is a viable question which deserves much thought and respect.

To begin, try by all means to avoid letting an attacker close to your person. Kicking and punching are more effective defenses (aside from talking, running and escaping) than wrestling, unless you are proficient in a martial art such as judo. This is why retaliatory defense must be swift, unyielding, powerful, concentrated and repetitive until the attacker is totally disabled — not just stunned or knocked down or pushed away. You don't want to be drawn into a wrestling match.

If you *are* forced to fight in-close, however, there are a number of things you can do to protect yourself. But, struggling *against* an attacker is usually a fruitless venture because men are most usually stronger than women. By struggling and wrestling, you may become tired, pull a muscle, strain yourself, or irritate the attacker with an annoying scratch or poke that only serves to anger him further. So, before employing any grappling technique, be sure to understand that this is the first step in a series of defenses and not a total defense in and of itself.

Let's approach this subject of grappling with one main thought: The human joints and tendons are not made to go in all directions; therefore, if you apply a properly executed grappling technique, you will be bending, twisting, pulling or pushing your opponent's joints and tendons in unnatural positions. By doing so, you will be creating pain as well as a condition whereby it is no longer humanly possible to hold onto you. The Chinese martial art known as Chin Na, or "grabbing and controlling," as well as the Japanese Jujitsu and Aikido and the Korean Hapkido, all teach techniques to seize the opponent and take control over him. These techniques require that your opponent is not forewarned that you are going to seize and control him. Therefore, never reach or go out of your way to grasp someone — the technique must be in the context of the given situation.

If your attacker reaches his arm around your neck and over your shoulder (fig. 21, a, b, c, d and e), move quickly and raise your arm which is closest to him straight

**fig. 21**
**a.**
**Defense against**
**a hug around**
**the neck.**

fig. 21a

### 21b

...reach your arm between yourself and your attacker (you may opt to attack his groin or continue through with this defense), behind his triceps and push forward with your body, using your arm as a rigid bar...

### 21c

...maintain your balance and do not go down with him as he is bent forward and is driven to the floor...

up between your bodies and behind his triceps. Then push him forward with your arm and body so that he bends

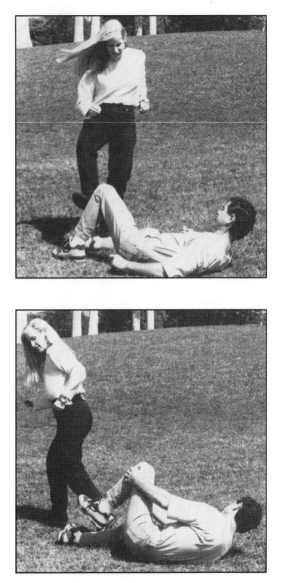

**fig. 21d**

...when he is down, quickly strike his shin or face with a definitive, hard kick or two before he can regain his balance and composure. If you strike to the knee or shin with enough force, he will not be able to get back on his feet.

downward, releasing his grasp.

In countering holds on your wrists, you will want to

escape by exploiting the gap between the opponent's thumb and index finger. If your attacker grabs your wrist, do not attempt to pull away, but instead, first strike him with your foot (on the shin) or fist (to the face or groin). Then, almost simultaneously, in a circular motion, using your hand, wrist and arm in the action, rotate your hand in a clockwise or counterclockwise direction until you are released (fig 22 a, b, c, d). The strike prior to the execution of the escape

**WRIST ESCAPE**
**When an attacker grabs your wrist...**

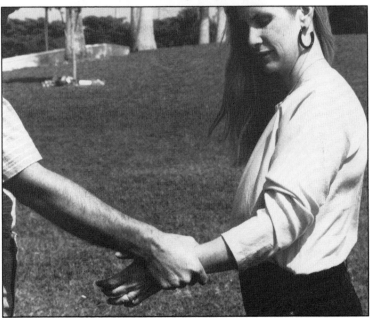

fig. 22a

technique cannot be understated here, because, when you strike your opponent, you distract him and cause his chi to

**...open your hand then rotate your wrist and hand while circling with your arm to loosen the attacker's grasp.**

fig. 22b

be dispersed, taking his strength away from his grasp.

Another way to escape from a hold, depending on the position of the offender, is to pry the little finger and bend it backward, against its natural range of motion (fig. 24). Or, you may use the fingernail press (fig. 23). To apply the fingernail press, dig the tip of your fingernail into the fingerrnail of the attacker, right at the juncture between the cuticle and the fingernail. Try this on yourself until you find

## fig. 22c & 22d

...continue circling, with your elbow bent until you are free.

the point where this causes excruciating pain. This defense is effective on any fingernail or toenail (fig. 23).

**FINGERNAIL PRESS.**
By squeezing or biting on the attacker's fingernail, with the force delivered toward the tip of the finger, where the cuticle meets the nail, excruciating results. To discover the right spot, practice this on yourself.

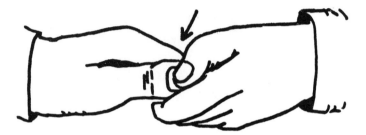

fig. 23

In the event of a hug from behind your back (fig. 24), there are several options available to you. First, you may attack the groin or grasp and twist the inner thigh of the attacker. These are both sensitive areas. You may also stomp on his foot or kick his shin with your heel. To free yourself from his grasp, take a step to the side into a wide, lower stance, with your knees slightly bent and your back straight. This puts the attacker off balance. At this instance, you may reach for his exposed groin and strike or squeeze. At the same time, you can grasp his little finger and bend it away as you escape. Once you escape, you must continue to punch and kick in combinations until you neutralize the attacker.

**Escape from a hug from behind.**

fig. 24a

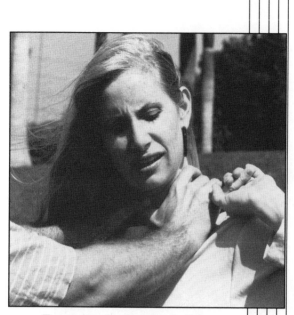

**To remove a hand, grasp the little finger and peel it back, in the opposite direction to which it naturally bends.**

fig. 24b

# CHAPTER NINE

# Stretching & Warm-up Exercises

The benefits of stretching the tendons with basic exercises are many-fold. Especially if you are a novice or "out of shape," it is very easy to pull a muscle or injure yourself in some other way without a thorough warm-up routine. Even

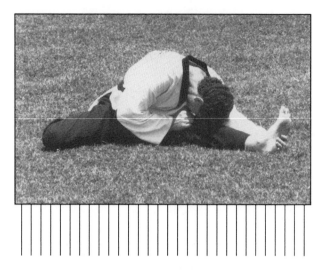

the greatest martial artists in the world are wise enough to engage in warm-up exercises before they practice their techniques.

Warming up with stretching exercises accomplishes several major objectives. Stretching loosens up stiff joints and tendons, lessening the chance of injury. Also, stretching strengthens muscles. And, stretching increases the elasticity of your tendons, allowing you greater range of motion, with higher, faster kicking. Women have a major advantage here over men, as they naturally possess a better stretch. Nor are women likely to be as muscle-bound. (Muscle mass hampers range of motion, decreases speed and restricts chi flow).

There are a number of simple stretches you can perform, starting from your head and working down to your toes. All stretching and warm-up exercises should be slow and without jerking or bouncing motions, with about eight to ten repetitions.

To stretch the neck, slowly turn your head from left to right as if watching a tennis match. Next, move your head up and down, nodding far forward then far back with your mouth closed.

To stretch your shoulders and back, perform large circles, front and back, with your arms. Next, with legs shoulder width apart and arms extended to the sides, twist slowly to the left then back to the right, turning as far as you comfortably can in each direction.

Placing your hands on your hips, rotate your hips,

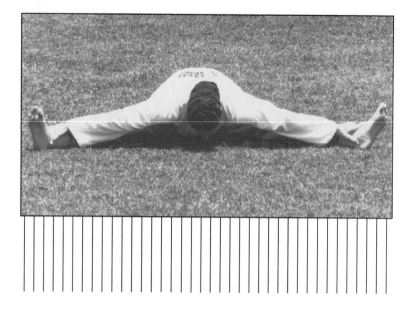

extending your pelvis forward then backward as you continue in a circular motion in one direction for one set, then the other direction for the next set.

To stretch the legs, with feet a bit wider than shoulder width, and legs straight, bend forward until the palms of your hands touch the floor. Hold for two counts then repeat.

In a seated position on the floor, put your legs, fully extended with locked knees, directly out in front of you then stretch forward as far as you can until your head rests on your legs. Hold for two counts then repeat.

Next, fold your right leg up so that the sole of the foot is resting against the inside thigh of the left leg. In this position, lean as far forward as you can over the left leg. Hold for two counts then repeat. Following this, repeat the exercise for the other leg.

To better stretch the knees and inner thighs, spread your legs as far apart as you can while sitting upright; then, with your back straight, lean as far forward as possible, touching your head to the floor. Hold for two counts. Next, touch your head to your right leg, then to the left leg. Repeat this process eight times, keeping your legs as widely spread apart as you can.

There are many more exercises to enhance your warm-up routine, including sit-ups, push-ups, jumping jacks, jumping in place, windmills, wrist and ankle rotations, etc. You may add these to your regimen as time and flexibility permit.

# CHAPTER TEN
# Exercising &
# Controlling the Mind

**If you study no other chapter in this book, this is the most important one to pay attention to.**

Most martial artists today, if asked what is the most effective form of self defense, would most likely tell you that it is a well-placed kick or punch. Under the close direction and tutelage of a master, you would find a very different answer — an answer that has been hidden away since the martial arts left the Orient. **The most effective form of self defense is control of the mind.**

When speaking of controlling the mind, we are dealing mainly with controlling your own mind, not the minds of others. With mind control, you can use your mind instead of having your mind use you; increase awareness; send chi (or vital energy) to parts of your body; direct chi to another's body; achieve clarity of thought and decision-making; and more. One who masters the art of controlling his/her mind may never need to fight.

## WHAT IS THE MIND?

The concept of using one's mind as a tool is new to the Western world, whereas in the East, it is not a concept at all, but rather a way of life. This is a significant distinction. As Westerners, we have to change our attitudes and undo a lifetime of cultural and social conditioning if we are to even come close to approaching this bottomless well known as the potential and capability of the mind. We have to look at things differently, as if in a child-like state of wonder and interest, without pre-conceived notions of what is "humanly" possible and what is "fantasy" or "imagination." We must redefine our sense of reality to delve into this subject matter, as we are not talking about philosophy or abstract notions, but rather worlds of existence that have been traditionally outside the boundaries of Western religious thought. If you are not willing to approach this subject of spirituality with an open mind, you will not be able to make it a reality for you.

In simplified terms, the mind is a tool which allows an individual to control his/her body and the influences upon it. Beyond the mind is spirit, or the essence of life. Some religions refer to this spirit as soul. Some people call this spirit "energy" and realize that it is electro-magnetic in composition — IT IS THE CHI which flows through our body. Many people, including Eastern religionists, believe

that we are energy, or Soul, which inhabits a human body —
we are not physical beings, but rather spiritual beings. As
such, spirit, or the essence of who we are, can be used to
direct the mind. The mind, under the direction of spirit, can
be used as a tool to perform for us.

To take this one step further, if the mind is not under
the control of spirit, it runs rampant, out of control, and
creates problems, falling victim to what some Eastern
philosophies call "the passions of the mind." These passions
include anger, lust, vanity, attachment and greed — these are
all caused by out-of-control minds.

The out-of-control mind is analogous to a machine
left to run without its operator; the machine jumps off the
work bench and leaves a wake of destruction in its wild path.
Eventually, this destruction will have to be paid for by the
operator and teaches him a lesson never to leave the machine
out of control again. The destruction, following the line of
this analogy, is referred to as Karma, the law of cause and
effect. According to some belief systems, if the "operator"
does not realize his/her fault in letting the mind run rampant
and pay for the "damages," this debt (also called "karmic
debt") will be carried on until it is indeed eventually paid for,
even if the hour of payment extends into subsequent lifetimes.
Since spirit or soul is non-physical and immortal, it must
reincarnate or take another body to pay off these debts and
learn how to live life without creating any more karma.

At this point, you may be asking, what in the world
does this have to do with martial arts? The answer is simple:
If you realize the nature of spirit, you realize the potential of
controlling the mind and making it work *for* you instead of
against you. Furthermore, you may learn to direct your chi
by using your mind. You also have the potential to increase

your awareness with exercises that rise beyond the mind. And, by controlling the mind, you will eliminate much of the unnecessary effects caused by letting it run on its own wild course. Exercises for the mind, over time, quiet the incessant chattering of the mind. If you have never meditated, you will find that it is very difficult to still the mind and make it quiet; this is because it is running rampant on its own accord. But, with time and persistence you will be able to regain control and achieve persistent clarity of the mind.

## MEDITATIVE EXERCISES

In martial arts in the Western world, physical exercise is highly regarded as the route to mastership. However, Easterners know differently. The road to mastership and full realization comes only by gaining clarity of the mind as the

first step. Without emphasis on controlling the mind and using it as a tool, there is an imbalance, creating an external-only art.

Every physical undertaking is precipitated by a mental action when we are first learning a technique. If you want to kick or punch, your mind must be engaged to tell your body how. If you want to paint a picture, your mind must be engaged to envision it first. Once control of the mind is realized, we may act more automatically in achieving our goals. In other words, we may act positively "without thinking." Note the difference between acting positively without thinking and acting negatively without thinking. The only differentiation is the degree to which mind is trained. One way of training the mind to listen is to keep it from talking and let it relax. This is the goal of meditation.

According to Tai Chi Chuan Master Da Liu, "In order to restore and rejuvenate the body, mind and spirit, one must cultivate the harmony of the total being within oneself and between oneself and the universe. The secret of chi cultivation is the practice of meditation, or mind relaxation. A relaxed mind is a necessary ingredient for a relaxed body. Then the spirit will become correspondingly relaxed.

"The secret of successful meditation is regularity, like the watering of plants or the human intake of food. Perseverance, diligence, and quiet determination are its nutritional ingredients. If it is done daily, continuous improvement can be expected. It is not a process that can be hurried. Do not expect instant success."[10]

## HOW DO YOU MEDITATE?

For twenty minutes, in a quiet, dimly lit room of moderate temperature, in the early morning or evening, sit with your eyes closed, breathing naturally. As you progress, over time, your breathing rate will slow down, in accord with your overall state of relaxation. Breathing should be concentrated in the abdomen.

"A baby breathes from the abdomen, an adult from the chest, an elderly person from the throat, and a dying man from the mouth. The more the muscles of the trunk — including the chest, diaphragm, rib cage, and abdominal muscles — are used for breathing, the more the lungs are provided with fresh air and the elasticity of the body maintained or restored.

"Good health, a sound mind in a sound body, and longevity are among the rewards derived from daily, meditative practice and breath-and-mind control is a hallmark of all of the Far Eastern religions and martial arts."[11]

Sitting on a cushion a couple inches high, cross your legs with one foot resting on the calf of the opposite leg and the other foot beneath the opposing calf. Allow your body to relax without slumping. The head, neck and trunk should remain vertically aligned, with the flow of gravity. Keep your lower back vertical, with the upper torso resting on the lumbar region.

Mentally, place your attention on the lower Dan Tien (the area a couple inches below the navel) where the body's chi should be concentrated. Touch your tongue to the roof of your mouth and keep your mouth and jaw relaxed, not clenched shut. With long, deep breaths, inhale and exhale a few times to oxygenate your lungs, respiratory, muscular, cardiovascular and circulatory systems. Then let your eyes, half-closed, fix upon some stationary point on the floor in a relaxed gaze. Natural blinking is okay.

Next, with your attention focused on your lower

abdomen, inhale through the nostrils, drawing the breath all the way into the lower abdomen before exhaling gently through both nostrils and open mouth. A breathing rate of eight cycles per minute is a good goal.

According to Master Da Liu, "The cultivation of harmony or chi cannot be, by its very nature, purely physical or purely mental. Meditation relaxes the emotional mind, which is the cause of physical tension." Thus we see the internal (mental) aspect as it relates to the external (physical) aspect of harmony. With repeated, persistent and disciplined meditative practice, you will continually reap the rewards of a more balanced state of being. Fifteen or twenty minutes of meditation a day is a minimal duration of practice. However, many practitioners meditate up to three hours or more, spread out over the course of a day.

Since mind stills the emotions, one of the greatest benefits is a clear mind. In terms of self defense, problem-solving, facing conflicts, managing stress or dealing with decision-making, a clear mind is the best tool you can have. You may never have to engage in a physical encounter at all if your mental acuity allows you to see danger before it enters your space. This is the greatest form of self defense.

## SPIRITUAL EXERCISES

Spiritual exercises, like meditation, are practiced to rise above the emotional body and above the mind. Whereas meditation seeks to still the "emotional" mind, the key to successful practice of spiritual exercises is the use of the imaginative faculty. After stilling the emotional mind, the spiritual exercise is used to create a mental image of a person or place until it becomes real and envelopes you so that you are now in another reality, or another plane of existence.

In the spiritual exercise, the person who contemplates

puts his attention on the "third eye," or spot between the physical eyes just above the bridge of the nose. The purpose of the spiritual exercise is to increase and improve awareness with the ultimate goal of mastering yourself as a spiritual being. This is not to say that anyone has ever learned all there is to learn and can go no further as a spiritual being, but rather that one learns to control the emotions and achieve a detached state even in the midst of a turbulent environment. Through the spiritual exercises, the practitioner is in a constant state of unfoldment — in and out of contemplation— climbing higher and higher into new and expanded states of awareness. Old notions give way to new ones and what you once thought you knew, you now understand in another light.

There are several ways to perform a spiritual exercise. Begin by finding a comfortable place, away from external distractions, either sitting up or lying down, and gently close your eyes, placing your attention on the blank screen between your eyes. Next, imagine a scene to your liking. Imagine it in detail, involving your "inner" senses. If it is a park, for instance, imagine the leaves in the trees. See the blades of grass as the breeze blows across them. Hear the birds chirping and smell the flowers. Fill your senses with the sights, sounds, odors, tastes and feelings within the visualization. With enough experience and practice, you will be able to make this scene a reality, ignoring the very existence of your physical body sitting in contemplation, as if asleep and in a dream. The difference is that you will be in a state of conscious awareness, acting as a creator and not a helpless bystander. In this altered state of being, you will be able to expand your awareness and realize a greater understanding of who you are and your relationship to the world around you.

Another spiritual exercise may begin in the same way as the first — by sitting in quiet comfort staring at the third eye. Chant the word HU (pronounced like the man's name Hugh) for several minutes, stilling your mind and looking for the light which is the gateway to the inner worlds of consciousness. The sound HU has a vibration which, when concentrated upon, raises the consciousness into a higher state.

"When all the outer world has been closed out, and even in the inner world of our thoughts our attention is fixed unwaveringly at the Tisra Til [the third eye], then we are ready to step across the invisible veil between the objective and subjective worlds. We should lose all feeling and sensation of the existence of the body...

"We look out through this door at the other worlds like a child who stays by a window watching the birds in the garden. His longing and hope to get through the window and play in the garden is magnified by his own imagination of what pleasures await him outside."[12]

With enough practice, the spiritual exercise will yield fascinating results. Many practitioners claim to see and meet with spiritual masters, visit temples on other planes, learn lessons on the meaning of life, and so on. As in meditation, the road to success rests upon keeping yourself on a disciplined schedule of practice.

Exercises which give you the ability to surpass and bypass the emotions have a ripple effect, sending waves of benefits to every dimension of your life, including increased awareness while awake, asleep or in contemplation, clarity of thought, ability to recognize "signs" of danger or confirmation, new patience and understanding of others, humility, and more. Eventually, you will achieve a detached state, or a state of neutrality in which you do not judge people or situations, or assume an emotional bias, but rather see the world from a standpoint of indifference. This is not to say that you do not *care* about anything, but rather that you take control over how things affect you and whether they are important enough to affect you.

The goal of these exercises is to create a more balanced "you" so that you can live with greater purpose and fulfillment, conquering the "lower self," the emotional body. As human beings, we are only balanced if our attention is distributed

**Meditative posture.**

evenly between spiritual, mental and physical pursuits. Over indulgence in any of these creates an imbalance.

The subject of mind, body and spirit is vast and inclusive of many factors ranging from states of consciousness and planes of existence to sound and light and the meaning of life itself. These matters must be studied and pursued with interest in order for you to fully realize your potential as a spiritual, as well as physical, being. If you are so inclined to include meditative or spiritual exercises in your daily schedule, you will grow in infinite ways.

## LIVING IN THE 'NOW'

With clarity of thought resulting from mental or spiritual exercise, you are able to "live in the now," which means that you can concentrate on the situation at hand. This applies not only to martial arts, but every other pursuit in your life. Your attention is best placed with full focus on what you are doing at the given moment.

If you are confronted by an attacker, you will be most effective in defending yourself if you are fully focused on the matter before you. Your full attention will block out your fear or any other emotion because your mind will have been trained to take control. If you become proficient enough in your spiritual or meditative exercises, you will not automatically judge the situation and guess what your opponent will do. Nor will you be intimidated by his yelling, his insults or his threats. You will only react when attacked and not be forced into overreacting or acting out of fear or anger.

When fear grips the emotional body, any number of things may happen — you could become trapped in a physical sense, you could freeze, you could panic, you could rise up in anger, you could break down from an emotional overload, etc. When you have control over your emotions, you become indifferent to the emotional body. The real you is in control and the real you will make the right choice of defense, whether it means striking back, running away, calling out for help, or totally avoiding a confrontation in the first place with some fast, smart thinking.

A number of years ago, the author was present when an uncommon occurrence took place at a Tae Kwon Do (Korean karate) school. Two of the students, both higher ranked individuals, got into a fight which ended up in the alley behind the school. In the course of the fight, both participants were so "keyed up" with emotion that each fought as if they never spent a day in a martial arts school. Neither fighter used a single technique they had learned in their years of training — both were too preoccupied with emotion to remember or have the presence of mind to draw upon their physical training. This served as an excellent reminder of what the martial arts mean with all physical training and no mental or spiritual training.

## MENTAL AWARENESS

Awareness is enlightenment — seeing and knowing things that have always been in existence, yet have now been drawn into your scope of recognition. You can add to this measure of awareness by practicing the art of observation, which is simply a matter of studying the world around you.

Notice the way people carry themselves. Look at whether people around you are balanced, how they stand, how they shift their weight. Notice how most people who become upset usually let their breathing rise into their chests and how they contract their muscles. Notice that you do the same thing. Become aware of how some people may be "disarmed" from being upset through diplomatic discussion. Observe what key words upset people and how they react. See how some people act out of power while others act out of consideration and respect. Watch how people use their body language and hands to threaten or retreat. Take note of what facial expressions precipitate a physical action.

The fine art of observing people gives you an insight into what to expect during a confrontation. You can tell whether someone is intoxicated, irrational, insecure or angry. You may also learn to recognize "abnormal" behavior.

With enough training in mental awareness, your fear over what might happen to you will give way to placing your attention on your opponent. This will enable you to recognize signs and afford you a mental and physical advantage.

You may expand your attention to visually explore your surroundings, finding an escape route, finding a weapon to defend yourself, finding and pulling on a fire alarm, creating a diversion, etc. Your mind is your greatest tool for self defense, but just like your body, it must be exercised and trained.

# CHAPTER ELEVEN
# Common Sense
# & Personal Safety

The best way to win a confrontation is never having to fight at all. And the best way to stay out of trouble is to avoid it. These words may sound simple, but the truth is, people tend to live dangerously and inadvertently place themselves in harm's way. Criminals are lazy people looking for an easy score. If you leave your doors and windows unlocked, you make an easier target than someone who is harder to access. This is common sense. With the expansion of awareness, as discussed in the previous chapter, you will increase your perception of *you*. In other words, you'll be able to pay attention to the things that you do which used to be out of habit or on a kind of "automatic pilot." You'll pay more attention to how you carry your purse or where you park your car and who may be watching you and how to distinguish between a glance which indicates an innocent physical attraction and a look which is threatening in nature.

In this chapter, we will examine some typical situations in which you can use your common sense to decrease your chances of being the victim of a personal crime.

## IN YOUR CAR
As members of a busy, active society, most suburbanites spend a lot of time in their automobiles. However, too many people take for granted that we are safe in our own, personal environment while behind the steering wheel. You'll notice

people in their cars acting as if they are all alone at home with not another soul watching them — as if they are invisible — oblivious to the world. Just take a look around you when you stop at a traffic light. It's amazing what a diversity of sights you see — women putting on makeup, men combing their hair, teenagers staring into the rear view mirror, people dancing in their seats to blasting car stereos or staring at and picking their teeth, drivers talking to themselves, and so on. So the question is: Are you aware of your environment while you are in your car, or are you one of those thousands, lost in your own world?

## DIRTY TRICKS

There's a long list of dirty tricks that criminals use to attack drivers. Most of these involve "setting up" the motorist, like using the proverbial "one-two" punch. One of the tricks is perpetrated when the criminal purposely drives his car into the back of his victim's vehicle. When the victim steps out of her car to assess the damages, she is mugged. Whether you stop and get out of your car for one of these set-ups should depend on a few factors — the time of day, how crowded the street is, how bad the "accident" is and your personal intuition.

Another trick used on the road to set up a mugging is the use of a flashing blue light by the criminal to pull women motorists over. We have become conditioned to pull over at the sight of a flashing light because we want to be law abiding citizens. Criminals aim to capitalize on this patriotism by impersonating "unmarked" police vehicles. If you are pulled over, take into consideration the above factors and, instead of stopping and getting out of your vehicle, stay on well-lit, busy streets until you drive yourself to the nearest police station. If the person is really a police officer in the other vehicle, he will have a "loud speaker" and be able to communicate to you with this device. And, if he's for real, he may even call for back-up, which would bring a marked police vehicle to the scene.

## SMASH & GRAB

"Smash and grab" is a term that has by now become a cliche in police terminology. It refers to any number of crimes wherein a criminal approaches the vehicle on foot, breaks the side window and mugs the occupants. Smash and grabs are very common at intersections and heavy traffic pile-ups where victims are hemmed in between the car in front of them and the one in back. When you have to stop in traffic, leave some room between you and the vehicle in front so you may have the option of quickly pulling into another lane or creating some other sort of diversion. If at all possible, do not get stuck in the center lane between four cars or between three cars and oncoming traffic in the next lane. This way, you may leave yourself an escape route over the curb and off to safety.

It is important to note here that **you must decide the absolute value of the contents of your purse, personal affects or jewelry vs. your personal safety or the safety of your passengers.** The old adage rings true, stating, "I'd rather give up my purse than to be stabbed or shot — the items in my purse can all be replaced."

If a criminal has a choice between breaking someone's window and robbing the motorist or reaching into an open window, he'll usually choose the second option. Fresh air is nice, but in traffic, you may want to opt for closing your windows and using the air conditioning.

95

## MAINTAINING YOUR VEHICLE

Your car should get you where you want to go without the hassle of breaking down for any reason. It is less expensive to keep up maintenance on your automobile than it is to suffer the myriad results of breaking down. The easiest thing to do is to make sure you always have enough gasoline, oil and water/coolant in the car. If you are going a long distance, driving on crowded streets or going to an unfamiliar destination, the last thing you want to do is underestimate how much gasoline you will be burning up on your trip. And you don't want your vehicle to overheat. Also, be sure to have your fan belts checked and replaced when worn. Other faulty and worn vehicle parts which can leave you stranded

include spark plugs and wires, battery, starter, switches, water pump, tires, hoses, etc. There are many parts of your car which may need replacing, but you especially want to take care of those which can disable the vehicle.

For safe measure, learn how to change your own tires, carry jumper cables and always let a friend or relative know where you are going.

By the way, there is an item on the market which fixes most types of flat tires in cases of emergency. The product is in the form of a spray can and features a head which screws into the tire valve. By depressing the top of the can, just as you would use a can of insecticide, the product is designed to inflate your tire and repair the leak long enough for you to make it to the next stop without having to even remove your tire in the first place. Sold under a number of brand names, the product can be found in auto stores and a wide variety of outlets, including many food stores. Similarly, there is a type of tape that is sold which can be used to quickly and easily repair a split water hose under the hood in the case of an emergency.

Lastly, while on the subject of helpful tools, if you can afford one, you may want to consider purchasing a mobile telephone. If you are in trouble, you can call for the police without leaving your vehicle.

## DECREASING THE CHANCES

Decreasing the chances of becoming a crime victim may be simpler than you think, if you consider the statistics. If you read the newspaper or pay attention to word of mouth, you'll have a pretty good idea of which neighborhoods you should avoid. Don't take the chance of traveling through unfamiliar areas, especially at night.

## THE WORLD OF ILLUSION

How many times have we heard the phrase "don't judge a book by its cover?" Well, getting back to the benefits of practicing the mental and spiritual exercises referred to in the previous chapter, you'll realize that ours is a world of illusion. This concept exists on many levels, but on the superficial level, especially in the United States, we see the master illusionists at work every waking moment. On television we see commercials for products that look and work better on the screen than in person; we find foods that taste great but are of poor nutritional quality, we are sold on making purchasing decisions based on image rather than on substance, and we tend to judge people at first glance by the way they look. It is this last point that we should examine in the context of personal safety.

Do not be fooled or distracted by men who look "nice" just because they are well-dressed and well-groomed. Remember that Al Capone used to get his nails done on a regular basis. Trust is something that should be earned over time, not on a casual meeting at a night club or some other social engagement. Beware of people who are overly eager to help you to your car unless you know you are safe; and don't use the way they carry themselves or the way they dress as a measure of their character. If you were a criminal and you knew that people are more likely to trust a well-tailored man than a sloppily clad one, how would you dress?

If people could be judged by their appearances, as well as their roles and relationships, then we would have no such thing as incest, date rape, molestation or other crimes in which the victim is taken advantage of by trusting the person he/she is with. People who commit these types of crimes are demented enough to do the unthinkable by breaking the sacred bonds of trust to carry out their personal assault. Don't judge the book by its cover.

## NIGHT TIME, NOT THE RIGHT TIME

Have you ever wondered what makes the night time so different from the day time in relation to the way people act? Night time seems to bring out the wild side of human behavior and this is coincidental to the time of day. Some people are looking to leave their day behind and party the night away. Others are out for a change of pace. And still others are looking for nothing but trouble. When you combine these human conditions with the unseen forces of nature brought on by the gravitational pull of the moon and planets, you have a breeding ground for unusual activity.

Don't be in the wrong place at the wrong time. Ask yourself whether your trip to the grocery store for a few much-needed items can wait until the first thing in the morning when it is light out, or whether you should risk walking to and from your car in a dimly lit parking lot with fewer than normal people million about. If you must be out at night, find a few friends to walk you to your car, or have someone bring your car around for you so that you don't have to venture into the dark alone. If you are at a night club, observe who may be observing you, so that when you are walking out the door, you are not being followed. Quite often, "bouncers" are chivalrous enough (or driven by their own sense of machismo) to watch you to your car.

Take into consideration that, if you are working late, you may be walking out into a deserted parking lot with no one else around, especially in a commercial area where business activity has ceased and everyone else has gone home for the day.

Night time is crime time for many muggers — visibility is diminished, shadowy hiding places are plentiful and the element of surprise is on their side.

## SCREAMING ATTACKERS

In most cases, an attacker who jumps out at his victim and screams, momentarily stunning him/her and at that very instance, creates a vulnerable opening for a successful attack. Many martial arts schools practice by yelling in class. To a large degree, as a student, you can get used to otherwise frightening screams and eventually not become unnerved by them. In fact, you can learn how to emit your own ear-deafening scream and turn the tables by shocking the attacker and throwing him off guard.

Wild animals, including dogs and cats, will always growl or vocally lash out at their opponent, causing the latter to retreat or back down. With proficiency in the mental exercises listed in the earlier chapter, you should be able to bring back your inner balance even if you are suddenly unnerved by a yelling attacker. Furthermore, you can be assured that anyone who is yelling at you has an unbalanced *chi* and is more vulnerable than you to sustaining an injury, especially to his heart channels. (A back kick or side kick, struck to a lower target at an on-rushing attacker is an excellent defense; see fig. 12, page 43.)

## WHOSE FREEDOM?

As a final note on this overall issue of common sense; many women claim that they resent giving way to the threat of criminal assault by avoiding certain places or not going out at night. They insist on asserting their right to the pursuit of happiness and refuse to surrender their personal freedom to would-be criminals. While this is very noble, it is often foolish. If you are using your mind to avoid becoming a victim, it is you who is taking the upper hand. Certainly, it is unfair that criminals rule the night or the neighborhood in many instances, but this may be a fact of life that is better fought through the judicial and police system than via personal sacrifice.

## GUNS & OTHER WEAPONS

In record numbers these days, women are purchasing hand guns for protection. Without commenting directly about the use of firearms as self defense tools, it should be noted that guns demand responsible behavior on the part of their owners.

Anyone who owns a firearm should learn how to use it, the laws governing its use and carriage, how to keep the weapon from being taken away and used against you, how to avoid firing the weapon in the instance that your adrenaline is pumping, how to store the weapon, how to clean and inspect it safely, and a host of other disciplines incumbent upon its owner. These same responsibilities apply to guard dogs, mace, pepper spray and other aerosols, "zap sticks," knives, martial arts stars, etc. There are courses available in weapons handling in most cities which will not only make you safer from yourself and others, but will also give you a greater peace of mind and confidence.

## A MEDLEY OF ADDITIONAL COMMON SENSE TIPS

- Don't leave your electronic garage door opener remote in your vehicle if it is not being stored in your garage — if this device is stolen from your car, someone obtains easy access to your home through your garage.
- Don't jog at night, or at least take your dog with you.
- Don't tell strangers or delivery men that your dog doesn't bite.
- Feel free to call the police if you are suspicious of strange sounds or sights.
- Install an alarm system in your car and home.
- Leave lights on in your home so that you don't have to enter into darkness.
- Be careful not to become a creature of habit so that someone can memorize your schedule.
- Have your keys in-hand on your way to your vehicle.
- Park in well-lit areas, close to the building.
- Avoid walking past construction sites.
- Look people in the eyes.
- Never fear to strike sensitive areas on an attacker.
- Plan an escape route for yourself out of your home or the place you are staying in case of emergencies.
- Don't open your door for strangers, including police, without a third-party confirmation.
- Don't be talked into anything you feel uncomfortable about.
- Do not let a stranger into your personal space. If he violates this space, he has forfeited his right to being treated with common courtesy — defend yourself with confidence and without hesitation.
- Do not feel compassion for an attacker.
- Don't be paranoid — be practical.

# CHAPTER TWELVE
# Martial Arts Schools

Martial arts schools are diverse in number, instructors, styles, curriculum, teaching methodology and emphasis. There are schools which emphasize sparring and there are those that provide aerobic-like conditioning. If you have never enrolled in a martial arts school, you will probably be perplexed and unsure about how to judge whether the school is right for you.

Start by asking yourself a few questions, like what you want to get out of the instruction. Most people, believe it or not, make receiving a black belt their number one priority. As the author's Tae Kwon Do master says to these people, "If you want a black belt, go to the flea market — you can get a good one cheap. You can get any color belt you want." In many schools, belts are not even awarded because the emphasis is to become trained and knowledgeable, not to be goal-oriented towards promotion.

Some people join a martial arts school to enter into tournaments and win trophies. It is true that if you are good enough to win a trophy, you must be learning something of value in the realm of self defense. But, again, it is a matter of focus. If your reason for taking a martial art is to win a trophy, then you are in it for sport. This is okay, as long as you are honest with yourself. Tournament fighting is not as realistic as street fighting or practical self defense. While many of the techniques are applicable for both, tournaments are restrictive of the types of techniques that are "legal." For instance, most strikes to the head, face, back and legs are illegal in most tournaments. And, if you are in a karate tournament, you may be confined to kicking and punching in legal areas, without being allowed by the rules to employ throws, grappling techniques or grabbing and twisting moves. Likewise, if you are in a judo tournament, it may be illegal to employ kicks or punches. So, you see that tournament fighting is restrictive, whereas street fighting carries no set of rules.

Tournament fighting and controlled fighting against a controlled opponent is known as "sparring." Sparring in

**The Korean Flag is displayed at Tae Kwon Do martial arts schools**

most karate schools is analogous to boxing with the hands and the feet, yet the impact of the blows are "focused," or controlled to the point where there is little or no actual contact committed on the opponent's person. This no-contact or light-contact sparring allows the practitioner to practice attacks and counterattacks, over and over in the course of a round. Protective padding, a mouthpiece and headgear are worn during full contact (tournament fighting) or medium contact sparring (practiced in many schools). Many women prefer not to engage in anything more than light contact or no-contact sparring, because of the potential of unsightly bruises or slight pain resulting from being struck. If this is the case with you, simply discuss this concern with the instructor before joining the school and find out whether you can participate in sparring on a more limited basis.

## FORMS

Another aspect of martial arts which is taught in most martial arts schools is the form, known in Japanese as "kata," and in Korean as "poomsee." Forms are pre-determined sets of techniques which the practitioner performs against an imaginary opponent. Forms were originally developed so that the practitioner could remember, practice and perfect a series of martial movements. It is an irony that forms are looked upon by so many martial arts students (especially novices) as an insignificant part of the overall art. Forms, in fact, carry the secrets of the martial arts. Each move in the form, from the bow at the beginning to the bow at the end, have a special meaning and purpose.

If you are trying to decide on a martial arts school to join, give great consideration to whether the school emphasizes forms. If at all possible, join a school with an advanced instructor who teaches the forms or who reviews them for correctness. Although any student can teach another a form, the more advanced the teacher, the more effective the form will be. A qualified teacher will know the intricacies of the form and whether the student is performing each move correctly with regard to speed, accuracy, stances, timing and

**Roundhouse kick to the kidney.**

power. Such an instructor will also know what each move in the form means and how it can be applied. There are many instructors, believe it or not, who do not know what the moves in their forms mean. If they don't know, how will you know how to practice them? When being taught a form, ask the instructor what each specific move is for.

## INSTRUCTORS

Unless you are taking a very specialized course in self defense which teaches only a few basic techniques, it is wise to find a school with a master instructor. Also, beware, because, there are many pseudo-masters running schools and claiming that they are masters, when, in fact, they are not. It's a good bet that if you go to a Tae Kwon Do school (Korean karate), and if the instructor is a Korean, and in good standing within his martial arts community, you can believe him when he claims that he is a master. The same holds true with a Chinese or Japanese instructor. There are many highly trained non-Asian martial arts instructors, but be skeptical about whether their title of "master" is real or contrived. Anyone can be checked out in terms of credentials, so take the proper time and do the research to ensure that you will be getting the expert training that you are paying for. If you ask the instructor about forms and he tells you that forms are not that important, or play a very little role in his "traditional" martial arts school, be particularly skeptical, because any bonafide instructor knows that the secrets to the martial arts movements are contained within the forms and not to recognize this is a tip-off that you may be at the wrong place for instruction.

Also, do not associate yourself with an instructor who borders on sadistic in his/her teaching methodology.

107

Although this may sound ridiculous, those who have been in the martial arts for a number of years have heard outlandish stories of certain instructors who like to shout at and abuse their students. These instructors have their students performing countless sets of push-ups, sit-ups or "toughening" exercises to make the student "tough" and "conditioned." Unless you are masochistic in your tendencies, you are at the school to learn self defense and self-discipline, not to be the object of someone's wrath. It's not difficult to recognize training techniques which are at direct odds with the spirit of the original martial arts. If the instructor is a mean person who intimidates his students, then he is acting out of power and you should find another school. If you are not given an explanation for what you are doing, or you find the exercise only remotely connected to learning self defense, then use your judgment and take yourself out of the situation. The martial arts, in their ancient origins, were built on respect for life, with controlling one's emotions as one of the highest attributes to be attained. This mind-set should be a part of the instructor's personality. If not, there is something wrong.

Lastly, do not be impressed by the number of trophies that are on display in the school. All of these trophies are usually not won by the instructor, but rather his students. Sometimes, the trophies are not even won by anybody related to that particular school, but left over, unclaimed, from past tournaments and they make impressive decorations. Pay more attention, if they are on exhibit in the school, to the awards and certificates on the walls which bear the instructor's name as the recipient.

## BASICS

"Basics" is a term which refers to basic techniques used in the martial arts. There is no substitute for learning the basics, which include basic kicks, stances and punches (covered in this book). With the proper instructor and with practice, the basic moves will provide the foundation for training. Basic punching, stances and kicking are similar in all martial arts styles and can be practiced on your own once you learn how to perform them correctly. Basics, as with any techniques, should be practiced in-place *as well as* while moving forward, backward and sideways. By practicing the basics, you will not only hone your performance of them, but you will also be working to enhance your balance, musculature and respiratory and circulatory systems. In many karate schools, basics and advanced techniques are vigorously performed while traversing the length of the exercise area, thus providing a great cardiovascular benefit.

## STEP SPARRING

Step sparring (also called one-step or two-step sparring) involves practicing attacks and counterattacks with a fellow student. One person attacks and the other counterattacks. For example, two students stand face to face in a fighting stance. One student throws a punch and the other student, as a counterattack, may block the punch and strike her opponent in the midsection or other target. These self defense drills build speed, accuracy, timing and awareness. For some reason, like forms, step sparring exercises are often underestimated by students in their importance. Perhaps this is because step sparring seems monotonous and too repetitive; or because there is nothing exciting about this practice. In any case, this is short-sighted thinking, as step sparring is very practical, offering students a controlled environment in which to practice defenses of many kinds against many kinds of strikes or kicks.

## DISCIPLINE

The concept of discipline in the martial arts school is most often misinterpreted, not only by students, but by many instructors as well. In our culture, discipline is frequently synonymous with punishment. But in the case of the martial arts, this is far off the mark. Discipline is not something that should be imposed by the instructor onto the student, but rather something that should be self-imposed. That is, a student should discipline herself to fully concentrate and train her mind to focus on what she is doing in the school, without a wandering mind and without interjecting thoughts which interfere with performing the technique or exercise at hand.

Discipline is not only relegated to the confines of the school itself, but should be incorporated into the student's life as a whole. Discipline involves training the mind, practicing awareness, learning to be responsible for your actions, being prepared, controlling your thoughts and more. As stated previously, if your instructor does not understand this concept of discipline, then he or she may a problem with power; and this may not be a good environment in which to learn.

## BOWING

In most martial arts schools, bowing is a tradition. This should not be confused with abusive behavior on the part of the instructor. On the contrary, bowing is a sign of recognition and respect, just as we are accustomed to shaking hands. Bowing does not denote subservience, nor is it an affront to one's religious or personal values. Out of sincerity and humbleness, bowing to the Korean, Chinese or Japanese flags shows respect to the origin of the martial art and acknowledgment with appreciation. People should not read anything more into the act of bowing than this.

# CHAPTER THIRTEEN
# Re-capping the Essentials

This book covers a lot of ground. However, there are a few concepts which bear repeating because of their innate importance:

**The greatest tool for self defense is your mind.** A clear, well-trained mind will keep you from freezing in the midst of a conflict. It can also make you aware enough to avoid confrontation and foster quick and good decision-making. With control over your mind, you will control your emotions, including fear, anger and attachment. Exercises to control the mind and make it work for you are essential not only to self-defense, but also to an enriched, enhanced life.

**Practice is the key to successful application.** Reading, studying, watching and discussing can only go so far in practicality. Anyone who desires to achieve a goal needs to practice sincerely, regularly and with precision. Practice brings wisdom borne of experience. Practice increases speed, endurance, power, accuracy, timing, balance and alertness.

**Live in harmony and balance.** Balance is the natural way of the universe. A balanced life style keeps us from overindulging, overexerting and ignoring other aspects of life that are important. The martial arts are based on a system of balance so that the practitioner learns to feed his/her sense of the physical, mental and spiritual.

**Find good instruction.** The techniques, concepts and practices discussed in this book will be best performed with a little experience under the tutelage of a qualified instructor. By learning the basics, you can practice on your own and add to your ability and skills.

**You are capable of defending yourself.** The strength and size of an opponent is a poor match for properly executed technique. Every opponent, by being human, is destructible and vulnerable in some way. With practice, you can act out of strength, with a clear mind.

**Be the "cause" in your life and not the "effect."** The spiritual law of cause and effect (called "karma" by the Easterners) dictates that every action (cause) creates a reaction (effect). By exercising your free will, you can create your own universe. Learn to avoid putting yourself in dangerous situations and to gain control over your life by gaining control over your mind, your emotions and your body. Practicing meditative or spiritual exercises can do this for you.

# Footnotes

1. *Flute of God*, by Paul Twitchell, ECKANKAR, Minneapolis, MN, page 141
2. *Dialogues with the Master*, by Paul Twitchell, ECKANKAR, Minneapolis, MN, page 29-30
3. *Chi Kung*, by Dr. Yang-Jwing Ming, Yang's Martial Arts Association (YMAA), Hong Kong, page 18
4. *Martial Arts, A Complete Illustrated History*, by Michael Finn, The Overlook Press, NY, page 14
5. *Kyusho-Jitsu: The Dillman Method of Pressure Point Fighting*, by George Dillman, A Dillman Karate International Book, page 37
6. ibid, page 37
7. ibid, page 38
8. *Chi Kung*, page 1
9. *Chi Kung*, page 8
10. *Taoist Health Exercise Book*, by Da Liu, Paragon House, New York, page 46
11. ibid, page 47
12. *Spiritual Notebook*, by Paul Twitchell, ECKANKAR, Minneapolis, MN, page 41

# Suggested Reading

The following books are helpful in learning more about martial arts, self defense, philosophy and spiritual expansion.

**Analysis of Shaolin Chin Na,** Dr. Yang Jwing-Ming, Yang's Martial Arts Association (YMAA), Hong Kong, 1991 (38 Hyde Park Avenue, Jamaica Plain, MA 02130). Ask for a complete list of volumes and tapes; also **Chi Kung, Health & Martial Arts.**

**Body Reflexology, Healing at Your Fingertips,** Mildred Carter, Parker Publishing Company, New York, 1983.

**Exploding the Myth of Self Defense,** Judith Fein, Ph.D., Torrance Publishing Company, P.O. Box 2558, Sabastopol, CA 95473, 1993.

**Fear Into Anger, A Manual of Self-Defense for Women**, Py Bateman, Nelson-Hall Paperback, Chicago, 1978.

**Kyusho-Jitsu: The Dillman Method of Pressure Point Fighting,** George A. Dillman, A Dillman Karate International Book, 1992 (251 Mountainview Road - Grill - Reading, PA 19607).

**Spiritual Notebook,** by Paul Twitchell, ECKANKAR, Minneapolis, MN, 1971.

**The Spiritual Laws of ECK,** by Harold Klemp, ECKANKAR, Minneapolis, MN, 1990.

**Tao of Jeet Kune Do,** by Bruce Lee, Ohara Publications, Santa Clarita, CA, 1975.

**Taoist Health Exercise Book,** by Da Liu, Paragon House, New York, NY 1991.